MAD LIBS®

MONSTER MASH
MAD LIBS

by Tristan Roarke

MAD LIBS
An Imprint of Penguin Random House LLC, New York

Mad Libs format and text copyright © 2021 by Penguin Random House LLC.
All rights reserved.

Concept created by Roger Price & Leonard Stern

Cover illustration by Scott Brooks

Published by Mad Libs,
an imprint of Penguin Random House LLC, New York.
Printed in the USA.

Visit us online at www.penguinrandomhouse.com.

ISBN 9780593225844
3 5 7 9 10 8 6 4 2

MAD LIBS

INSTRUCTIONS

MAD LIBS® is a game for people who don't like games!
It can be played by one, two, three, four, or forty.

• RIDICULOUSLY SIMPLE DIRECTIONS

In this tablet you will find stories containing blank spaces where words
are left out. One player, the READER, selects one of these stories. The
READER does not tell anyone what the story is about. Instead, he/she asks
the other players, the WRITERS, to give him/her words. These words are
used to fill in the blank spaces in the story.

• TO PLAY

The READER asks each WRITER in turn to call out a word—an adjective or
a noun or whatever the space calls for—and uses them to fill in the blank
spaces in the story. The result is a MAD LIBS® game.

When the READER then reads the completed MAD LIBS® game to the other
players, they will discover that they have written a story that is fantastic,
screamingly funny, shocking, silly, crazy, or just plain dumb—depending
upon which words each WRITER called out.

• EXAMPLE (*Before* and *After*)

"_____!" he said _____
      EXCLAMATION   ADVERB

as he jumped into his convertible _____ and
                                                  NOUN

drove off with his _____ wife.
                          ADJECTIVE

"**OUCH**!" he said **HAPPILY**
      EXCLAMATION   ADVERB

as he jumped into his convertible **CAT** and
                                              NOUN

drove off with his **BRAVE** wife.
                          ADJECTIVE

In case you have forgotten what adjectives, adverbs, nouns, and verbs are, here is a quick review:

An ADJECTIVE describes something or somebody. *Lumpy*, *soft*, *ugly*, *messy*, and *short* are adjectives.

An ADVERB tells how something is done. It modifies a verb and usually ends in "ly." *Modestly*, *stupidly*, *greedily*, and *carefully* are adverbs.

A NOUN is the name of a person, place, or thing. *Sidewalk*, *umbrella*, *bridle*, *bathtub*, and *nose* are nouns.

A VERB is an action word. *Run*, *pitch*, *jump*, and *swim* are verbs. Put the verbs in past tense if the directions say PAST TENSE. *Ran*, *pitched*, *jumped*, and *swam* are verbs in the past tense.

When we ask for A PLACE, we mean any sort of place: a country or city (*Spain*, *Cleveland*) or a room (*bathroom*, *kitchen*).

An EXCLAMATION or SILLY WORD is any sort of funny sound, gasp, grunt, or outcry, like *Wow!*, *Ouch!*, *Whomp!*, *Ick!*, and *Gadzooks!*

When we ask for specific words, like a NUMBER, a COLOR, an ANIMAL, or a PART OF THE BODY, we mean a word that is one of those things, like *seven*, *blue*, *horse*, or *head*.

When we ask for a PLURAL, it means more than one. For example, *cat* pluralized is *cats*.

MAD LIBS® is fun to play with friends, but you can also play it by yourself! To begin with, DO NOT look at the story on the page below. Fill in the blanks on this page with the words called for. Then, using the words you have selected, fill in the blank spaces in the story.

Now you've created your own hilarious MAD LIBS® game!

MONSTERS, OH MY!

NOUN _____

ADJECTIVE _____

TYPE OF LIQUID _____

SOMETHING ALIVE (PLURAL) _____

ANIMAL (PLURAL) _____

PLURAL NOUN _____

ADVERB _____

ARTICLE OF CLOTHING (PLURAL) _____

NUMBER _____

OCCUPATION (PLURAL) _____

NOUN _____

VERB ENDING IN "ING" _____

VERB _____

PLURAL NOUN _____

NOUN _____

VERB ENDING IN "ING" _____

OCCUPATION _____

MAD LIBS

MONSTERS, OH MY!

Have you ever heard a loud _____ in the middle of
NOUN

the night, when the moon is _____? Do you suspect
ADJECTIVE

your new neighbor might like to drink the _____
TYPE OF LIQUID

from _____? Undead zombies, howling
SOMETHING ALIVE (PLURAL)

were-_____, and vampires that sleep in _____
ANIMAL (PLURAL)   PLURAL NOUN

have _____ scared the _____ off
ADVERB   ARTICLE OF CLOTHING (PLURAL)

audiences for over _____ years. But what if these terrifying
NUMBER

_____ were real? What if they really *were* hiding under
OCCUPATION (PLURAL)

your _____, waiting until you're _____ before
NOUN   VERB ENDING IN "ING"

they sneak out and _____ you? Luckily, monsters are just
VERB

a figment of our _____. So next time you hear that
PLURAL NOUN

_____ in the night, relax! You're just _____
NOUN   VERB ENDING IN "ING"

things. There's no _____ under your bed, waiting to get
OCCUPATION

you . . . or is there?!

MAD LIBS® is fun to play with friends, but you can also play it by yourself! To begin with, DO NOT look at the story on the page below. Fill in the blanks on this page with the words called for. Then, using the words you have selected, fill in the blank spaces in the story.

Now you've created your own hilarious MAD LIBS® game!

MAN'S BEST FRIEND

ADJECTIVE _____

OCCUPATION _____

CELEBRITY _____

SOMETHING ALIVE _____

VERB (PAST TENSE) _____

PART OF THE BODY (PLURAL) _____

TYPE OF FOOD _____

VERB _____

NOUN _____

ADJECTIVE _____

SILLY WORD _____

VEHICLE _____

A PLACE _____

PART OF THE BODY _____

EXCLAMATION _____

NOUN _____

VERB _____

MAD LIBS®

MAN'S BEST FRIEND

Ever wonder what it's like to have a/an _____ zombie as a
ADJECTIVE

best _____? Well, wonder no more, because my best friend,
OCCUPATION

_____ , is a real-life zombie. Of course, she wasn't *always* a
CELEBRITY

zombie. She used to be a regular _____ before that other
SOMETHING ALIVE

zombie _____ on her leg. Being friends with a zombie
VERB (PAST TENSE)

sure does keep you on your _____ . I need to keep
PART OF THE BODY (PLURAL)

lots of fresh _____ close by to feed my zombie friend so she
TYPE OF FOOD

won't try to _____ my _____ . And our conversations
VERB   NOUN

aren't very _____ since my zombie friend usually just moans,
ADJECTIVE

" _____ ." At least she still likes to ride her _____
SILLY WORD   VEHICLE

around (the) _____ . Although, every time she rides over a
A PLACE

bump, her _____ falls off and she yells, " _____ !"
PART OF THE BODY   EXCLAMATION

But no matter what, she's still my best _____ friend
NOUN

forever . . . even if she's always trying to _____ on me.
VERB

MAD LIBS® is fun to play with friends, but you can also play it by yourself! To begin with, DO NOT look at the story on the page below. Fill in the blanks on this page with the words called for. Then, using the words you have selected, fill in the blank spaces in the story.

Now you've created your own hilarious MAD LIBS® game!

HOW TO MAKE A MONSTER

ADJECTIVE _____

SOMETHING ALIVE _____

A PLACE _____

ADJECTIVE _____

PLURAL NOUN _____

PART OF THE BODY (PLURAL) _____

NUMBER _____

PART OF THE BODY (PLURAL) _____

TYPE OF BUILDING _____

NOUN _____

NOUN _____

NOUN _____

VERB ENDING IN "ING" _____

OCCUPATION _____

EXCLAMATION _____

VERB _____

PERSON IN ROOM _____

ADJECTIVE _____

MAD LIBS

HOW TO MAKE A MONSTER

Hello, all my little _____ scientists! Dr. Frankenslime here
                          ADJECTIVE

to teach you how to make your own scary _____. The
                                          SOMETHING ALIVE

first thing you need to do is go to a creepy _____ with a/an
                                               A PLACE

_____ shovel and dig up all the _____ you
    ADJECTIVE   PLURAL NOUN

need for the project. Don't feel like you have to give your monster

two _____ and two legs. If you want to give it
      PART OF THE BODY (PLURAL)

_____ _____ instead, go for it! This is your
   NUMBER   PART OF THE BODY (PLURAL)

monster! Assemble all the parts in the laboratory inside your haunted

_____. If you don't have a lab, you can always use the
  TYPE OF BUILDING

_____ in your own home instead. Once your monster is
      NOUN

assembled, use an electrical _____ to bring it to life. A/An
                                 NOUN

_____ -storm is an excellent source of electricity due to all
      NOUN

the lightning bolts _____ from the sky. When your
                     VERB ENDING IN "ING"

_____ first sits up, it may shout, "_____!" and
   OCCUPATION   EXCLAMATION

_____ uncontrollably, but you must stay calm. Now all you
      VERB

have to do is give it a name, like "_____," and go show the
                                     PERSON IN ROOM

world your _____ creation!
              ADJECTIVE

MAD LIBS® is fun to play with friends, but you can also play it by yourself! To begin with, DO NOT look at the story on the page below. Fill in the blanks on this page with the words called for. Then, using the words you have selected, fill in the blank spaces in the story.

Now you've created your own hilarious MAD LIBS® game!

VAMPIRE CLASS

SILLY WORD _____

ADJECTIVE _____

NOUN _____

NOUN _____

TYPE OF CONTAINER _____

ADVERB _____

PLURAL NOUN _____

SOMETHING ALIVE _____

PART OF THE BODY _____

TYPE OF LIQUID _____

ANIMAL _____

PART OF THE BODY (PLURAL) _____

OCCUPATION _____

EXCLAMATION _____

PLURAL NOUN _____

SOMETHING ALIVE _____

PART OF THE BODY (PLURAL) _____

MAD LIBS®

VAMPIRE CLASS

Velcome to Count _____'s class on how to be a successful
                         SILLY WORD

vampire! These _____ tips vill tell you everythink you need
                    ADJECTIVE

to know about being a creature of the _____ .
                                            NOUN

Tip #1: Vampires hate the _____ , so never leave your
                                    NOUN

_____ during the day. One step into the sunlight and
TYPE OF CONTAINER

you'll be _____ turned into a pile of _____ .
              ADVERB   PLURAL NOUN

Tip #2: Before you bite your _____ on the _____ ,
                                  SOMETHING ALIVE   PART OF THE BODY

say, "I vant to suck your _____ !"
                            TYPE OF LIQUID

Tip #3: To transform into a flying _____ , just raise your
                                          ANIMAL

_____ into the air and say the _____'s
PART OF THE BODY (PLURAL)   OCCUPATION

phrase, " _____ ."
            EXCLAMATION

You are all excellent _____ ! Next, I vill teach you how to
                        PLURAL NOUN

hypnotize your _____ with your _____ .
                  SOMETHING ALIVE   PART OF THE BODY (PLURAL)

MAD LIBS® is fun to play with friends, but you can also play it by yourself! To begin with, DO NOT look at the story on the page below. Fill in the blanks on this page with the words called for. Then, using the words you have selected, fill in the blank spaces in the story.

Now you've created your own hilarious MAD LIBS® game!

WHAT LURKS IN LOCH NESS?

ADJECTIVE _____

NOUN _____

CELEBRITY _____

NUMBER _____

OCCUPATION _____

PERSON IN ROOM _____

SAME CELEBRITY _____

EXCLAMATION _____

ADJECTIVE _____

PLURAL NOUN _____

PART OF THE BODY _____

NUMBER _____

PLURAL NOUN _____

ADJECTIVE _____

ANIMAL _____

SILLY WORD _____

NOUN _____

ADJECTIVE _____

MAD LIBS®
WHAT LURKS IN
LOCH NESS?

If you ever travel to Scotland, you might be _____ enough to
ADJECTIVE

catch a glimpse of the Loch Ness _____, also affectionately
NOUN

known as _____ . Sightings of the creature date all the way
CELEBRITY

back to the year _____ when, legend has it, a/an _____
NUMBER   OCCUPATION

named _____ saw _____ rising from the lake and
PERSON IN ROOM   SAME CELEBRITY

shouted, "_____!" Since then, Loch Ness has been a/an
EXCLAMATION

_____ destination for _____ traveling from all
ADJECTIVE   PLURAL NOUN

over the world. The creature is said to have a/an _____
PART OF THE BODY

nearly _____ feet tall and a body longer than twenty
NUMBER

_____! While many think the legend is just a/an
PLURAL NOUN

_____ hoax, believers say the creature is actually some type of
ADJECTIVE

_____ that was trapped in the lake during the _____
ANIMAL   SILLY WORD

age. Whatever the truth may be, if you're lucky enough to take a photo

of the _____ , you'll become one of the most _____
NOUN   ADJECTIVE

people in the world!

MAD LIBS® is fun to play with friends, but you can also play it by yourself! To begin with, DO NOT look at the story on the page below. Fill in the blanks on this page with the words called for. Then, using the words you have selected, fill in the blank spaces in the story.

Now you've created your own hilarious MAD LIBS® game!

ARE YOU MY MUMMY?

ADJECTIVE _____

PLURAL NOUN _____

TYPE OF BUILDING _____

ARTICLE OF CLOTHING (PLURAL) _____

NOUN _____

NOUN _____

ADJECTIVE _____

PART OF THE BODY (PLURAL) _____

NOUN _____

SOMETHING ALIVE (PLURAL) _____

SILLY WORD _____

VERB _____

ADJECTIVE _____

TYPE OF CONTAINER _____

ANIMAL (PLURAL) _____

NUMBER _____

NOUN _____

MAD LIBS

ARE YOU MY MUMMY?

Is your mom a/an _____ mummy? Answer these helpful
ADJECTIVE

_____ to find out!
PLURAL NOUN

- Does your mom sleep inside a stone _____ while
TYPE OF BUILDING

  wrapped in _____ ?
ARTICLE OF CLOTHING (PLURAL)

- Does your mom come from a/an _____ in the middle
NOUN

  of a desert, where she creates _____ -storms by waving
NOUN

  around a/an _____ staff?
ADJECTIVE

- Does your mom keep her _____ in a/an
PART OF THE BODY (PLURAL)

  _____ by her bed?
NOUN

- When your _____ meet your mom, do they
SOMETHING ALIVE (PLURAL)

  scream, "_____ !" and _____ in fear?
SILLY WORD   VERB

- Does your mom have a pile of _____ treasure in your
ADJECTIVE

  _____ ?
TYPE OF CONTAINER

- After your mom hugs you, are you covered in scarab

  _____ ?
ANIMAL (PLURAL)

If you answered "yes" to more than _____ of these questions,
NUMBER

your mom might be a/an _____ !
NOUN

From MONSTER MASH MAD LIBS® • Copyright © 2021 by Penguin Random House LLC.

MAD LIBS® is fun to play with friends, but you can also play it by yourself! To begin with, DO NOT look at the story on the page below. Fill in the blanks on this page with the words called for. Then, using the words you have selected, fill in the blank spaces in the story.

Now you've created your own hilarious MAD LIBS® game!

DIARY FROM THE BLACK LAGOON

ADJECTIVE _____

SOMETHING ALIVE (PLURAL) _____

ADJECTIVE _____

SILLY WORD _____

PLURAL NOUN _____

EXCLAMATION _____

COLOR _____

PLURAL NOUN _____

PART OF THE BODY (PLURAL) _____

OCCUPATION _____

SOMETHING ALIVE (PLURAL) _____

ANIMAL _____

VERB ENDING IN "ING" _____

TYPE OF BUILDING _____

ADJECTIVE _____

VERB _____

PLURAL NOUN _____

ANIMAL (PLURAL) _____

MAD LIBS®
DIARY FROM
THE BLACK LAGOON

Dear Diary: It was another _____ day here at the lagoon. A
                                ADJECTIVE

couple of _____ came to swim. I thought it would
          SOMETHING ALIVE (PLURAL)

be a/an _____ idea to go say "_____" and make
        ADJECTIVE   SILLY WORD

friends. Of course, the moment they saw me rise out of the water

covered in _____, they screamed, "_____!
            PLURAL NOUN   EXCLAMATION

It's the creature of the _____ lagoon!" and ran away. I
                          COLOR

can't help it if I have _____ on my cheeks and webbed
                         PLURAL NOUN

_____. I have feelings just like any other
    PART OF THE BODY (PLURAL)

_____. I just wish _____ could see
   OCCUPATION   SOMETHING ALIVE (PLURAL)

me for the lonely _____ that I really am. My only friends
                    ANIMAL

are the fish _____ in the lake. I wish I could live inside
             VERB ENDING IN "ING"

a big _____ instead of a/an _____ lagoon like
      TYPE OF BUILDING   ADJECTIVE

this one. But until I do, I'll just have to _____ with the
                                              VERB

_____ living in here. At least they don't care that I smell
   PLURAL NOUN

like _____.
      ANIMAL (PLURAL)

MAD LIBS® is fun to play with friends, but you can also play it by yourself! To begin with, DO NOT look at the story on the page below. Fill in the blanks on this page with the words called for. Then, using the words you have selected, fill in the blank spaces in the story.

Now you've created your own hilarious MAD LIBS® game!

BIGFOOT

ADJECTIVE _____

PART OF THE BODY (PLURAL) _____

ADJECTIVE _____

VERB ENDING IN "ING" _____

NUMBER _____

NOUN _____

SOMETHING ALIVE _____

ADJECTIVE _____

PLURAL NOUN _____

CELEBRITY _____

SOMETHING ALIVE (PLURAL) _____

ADVERB _____

ADJECTIVE _____

PART OF THE BODY _____

OCCUPATION _____

ADJECTIVE _____

A PLACE _____

PLURAL NOUN _____

MAD LIBS

BIGFOOT

Hello. Me name is Sasquatch, but you may know me better as

_____ -foot. People call me that name because me
ADJECTIVE

_____ are very, very _____ . You may
PART OF THE BODY (PLURAL)   ADJECTIVE

have seen photos or videos of me _____ in the forest.
                                  VERB ENDING IN "ING"

If not, me tell you that me am _____ feet tall and me body is
                                NUMBER

covered in brown _____ like a/an _____ . Me
                  NOUN   SOMETHING ALIVE

favorite food is _____ _____ . Me am like the
                 ADJECTIVE   PLURAL NOUN

_____ of the forest because _____
CELEBRITY   SOMETHING ALIVE (PLURAL)

always trying to take picture of me to put on thing called internet. But

me always _____ run away before they can see me. Me also
           ADVERB

have cousin named _____-_____ . He just as tall
                  ADJECTIVE   PART OF THE BODY

as me and look like a big, hairy _____ . We not see each other
                                 OCCUPATION

too much because he even more _____ than me. Me hope
                              ADJECTIVE

you come visit (the) _____ where me live and we can go scare
                     A PLACE

all the _____ together!
        PLURAL NOUN

MAD LIBS® is fun to play with friends, but you can also play it by yourself! To begin with, DO NOT look at the story on the page below. Fill in the blanks on this page with the words called for. Then, using the words you have selected, fill in the blank spaces in the story.

Now you've created your own hilarious MAD LIBS® game!

HYDE AND DRINK

OCCUPATION _____

NOUN _____

ADJECTIVE _____

VERB _____

SOMETHING ALIVE _____

TYPE OF LIQUID _____

NOUN _____

ADJECTIVE _____

PLURAL NOUN _____

ADVERB _____

VERB _____

SILLY WORD _____

PLURAL NOUN _____

ADJECTIVE _____

PLURAL NOUN _____

NUMBER _____

ADJECTIVE _____

CELEBRITY _____

MAD LIBS®

HYDE AND DRINK

I am the world-famous _____ Dr. Jekyll! I created the
                         OCCUPATION

_____ that can turn me into the _____
        NOUN   ADJECTIVE

monster known as Mr. _____! Today, I'll teach you how
                            VERB

to make your very own potion that will turn you into a terrifying

_____ , just like me! First, you must boil _____
SOMETHING ALIVE   TYPE OF LIQUID

inside an old _____ until it smells quite _____ .
                    NOUN   ADJECTIVE

Next, get a handful of gooey _____ and _____
                                   PLURAL NOUN   ADVERB

mix them with the liquid until it starts to _____ . Lastly,
                                                   VERB

take some di-oxy-_____-ide and shake it as hard as you
                     SILLY WORD

can until you see _____ start to form inside, then mix
                        PLURAL NOUN

it with the other solution. Drink it if you dare, as it will taste like

_____ _____ . Now wait _____
     ADJECTIVE   PLURAL NOUN   NUMBER

minutes, and if you followed these instructions correctly, you'll turn

into a/an _____ monster called Mr. _____!
               ADJECTIVE   CELEBRITY

MAD LIBS® is fun to play with friends, but you can also play it by yourself! To begin with, DO NOT look at the story on the page below. Fill in the blanks on this page with the words called for. Then, using the words you have selected, fill in the blank spaces in the story.

Now you've created your own hilarious MAD LIBS® game!

TROLLING FOR GOBLINS

VERB ENDING IN "ING" _____

PLURAL NOUN _____

ADJECTIVE _____

ADJECTIVE _____

NOUN _____

NUMBER _____

SOMETHING ALIVE _____

PLURAL NOUN _____

PART OF THE BODY (PLURAL) _____

VEHICLE _____

A PLACE _____

NOUN _____

ARTICLE OF CLOTHING _____

VERB _____

NOUN _____

A PLACE _____

SOMETHING ALIVE (PLURAL) _____

ADVERB _____

TROLLING FOR GOBLINS

When you're _____ through the mountains or dense

VERB ENDING IN "ING"

_____ , you may encounter a troll or goblin, so it's very

PLURAL NOUN

_____ to know how to tell the difference! The first

ADJECTIVE

_____ difference you'll notice between a troll and a goblin

ADJECTIVE

is the size of the _____ . Trolls are almost _____

NOUN ... NUMBER

times bigger than goblins! Trolls are said to look very similar to a/an

_____ , while goblins have green skin and wild

SOMETHING ALIVE

_____ growing atop their _____ .

PLURAL NOUN ... PART OF THE BODY (PLURAL)

Trolls prefer to live under a/an _____ or under bridges,

VEHICLE

while goblins would rather live in (the) _____ . Perhaps

A PLACE

the most important difference is that a goblin will use their magical

_____ to steal your gold or _____ , whereas a

NOUN ... ARTICLE OF CLOTHING

troll may try to _____ you if they're hungry! Luckily, a troll

VERB

will turn into a/an _____ if they step into the sun, so always

NOUN

make sure it's sunny before you go hiking in (the) _____ .

A PLACE

Both goblins and trolls dislike _____ , so be

SOMETHING ALIVE (PLURAL)

_____ careful if you see one!

ADVERB

MAD LIBS® is fun to play with friends, but you can also play it by yourself! To begin with, DO NOT look at the story on the page below. Fill in the blanks on this page with the words called for. Then, using the words you have selected, fill in the blank spaces in the story.

Now you've created your own hilarious MAD LIBS® game!

CHEW ON THIS

SOMETHING ALIVE (PLURAL) _____

PLURAL NOUN _____

ADJECTIVE _____

VERB _____

PLURAL NOUN _____

ANIMAL _____

ADJECTIVE _____

PART OF THE BODY (PLURAL) _____

TYPE OF LIQUID _____

SOMETHING ALIVE (PLURAL) _____

SAME SOMETHING ALIVE (PLURAL) _____

TYPE OF FOOD (PLURAL) _____

NOUN _____

ANIMAL (PLURAL) _____

A PLACE _____

NOUN _____

OCCUPATION _____

MAD LIBS

CHEW ON THIS

Do your friends have boring pets like _____ or
SOMETHING ALIVE (PLURAL)

_____ ? If you've always wanted a/an _____-looking
PLURAL NOUN   ADJECTIVE

pet that'll make people _____ in fear, then a chupacabra is
VERB

perfect for you! Chupacabras are magical _____ known for
PLURAL NOUN

looking like a hairless _____ with _____ skin.
ANIMAL   ADJECTIVE

Chupacabras have very sharp _____ that they use
PART OF THE BODY (PLURAL)

to suck the _____ from _____
TYPE OF LIQUID   SOMETHING ALIVE (PLURAL)

when they're hungry. But don't worry if you don't have

_____ to feed your pet chupacabra. It'll be just
SAME SOMETHING ALIVE (PLURAL)

as happy if you let it eat a bag of _____ . Chupacabras
TYPE OF FOOD (PLURAL)

may not like playing normal pet games like fetch the _____ ,
NOUN

but they love chasing _____ around (the) _____ .
ANIMAL (PLURAL)   A PLACE

Sure, your pet chupacabra may mess up your _____ now and
NOUN

then, but that doesn't mean it won't love cuddling up with you! So have

fun with your new pet chupacabra. Just make sure it doesn't eat your

next-door _____ .
OCCUPATION

MAD LIBS® is fun to play with friends, but you can also play it by yourself! To begin with, DO NOT look at the story on the page below. Fill in the blanks on this page with the words called for. Then, using the words you have selected, fill in the blank spaces in the story.

Now you've created your own hilarious MAD LIBS® game!

OGRE AND OUT

LAST NAME _____

OCCUPATION _____

ADJECTIVE _____

EXCLAMATION _____

PLURAL NOUN _____

ADJECTIVE _____

ADJECTIVE _____

PLURAL NOUN _____

ANIMAL _____

NOUN _____

NOUN _____

ADVERB _____

SOMETHING ALIVE (PLURAL) _____

SILLY WORD _____

TYPE OF LIQUID _____

OCCUPATION _____

VERB _____

ADJECTIVE _____

MAD LIBS®

OGRE AND OUT

One day our principal, Mrs. _____ , came into our classroom
                                LAST NAME

and told us that we'd be having a substitute _____ for the rest
                                              OCCUPATION

of the school year. We were _____ when we saw an ogre walk
                             ADJECTIVE

into the classroom. "Hello, class! My name is Mr. _____ ,"
                                                   EXCLAMATION

he growled. "But you can call me ' _____ ' for short."
                                   PLURAL NOUN

Having an ogre as a substitute was the most _____
                                             ADJECTIVE

experience of my life! He had green skin, a/an _____ head,
                                                ADJECTIVE

and two long _____ sticking out of his mouth. He smelled
             PLURAL NOUN

like a/an _____ and carried a huge wooden _____
          ANIMAL   NOUN

that he would pound on the _____ every time he
                           NOUN

_____ laughed. His favorite subjects to teach were math and
ADVERB

"How to Scare the _____ that Live in the Village."
                  SOMETHING ALIVE (PLURAL)

Every day, he would greet us by saying "Fee-Fi-Fo- _____ ,
                                                    SILLY WORD

I smell the _____ of a/an _____ !" Then he'd
            TYPE OF LIQUID   OCCUPATION

say that if he was hungry, he'd _____ any student who
                                VERB

didn't turn in their homework. I think he was joking, but I was too

_____ to find out.
ADJECTIVE

MAD LIBS® is fun to play with friends, but you can also play it by yourself! To begin with, DO NOT look at the story on the page below. Fill in the blanks on this page with the words called for. Then, using the words you have selected, fill in the blank spaces in the story.

Now you've created your own hilarious MAD LIBS® game!

BUMP IN THE NIGHT

NOUN _____

PLURAL NOUN _____

TYPE OF BUILDING _____

VERB _____

PLURAL NOUN _____

SILLY WORD _____

PART OF THE BODY _____

NOUN _____

ANIMAL _____

NOUN _____

VERB ENDING IN "ING" _____

TYPE OF FOOD (PLURAL) _____

VERB _____

ADJECTIVE _____

TYPE OF LIQUID _____

EXCLAMATION _____

SOMETHING ALIVE _____

NOUN _____

MAD LIBS

BUMP IN THE NIGHT

Is there a creature living under your _____? Answer these
NOUN

_____ to find out if you're sharing your _____
PLURAL NOUN   TYPE OF BUILDING

with a monster!

- When you _____ at night, do you hear strange
  VERB

  _____ that sound like _____?
  PLURAL NOUN   SILLY WORD

- Have you ever seen a hairy _____ reaching out from
  PART OF THE BODY

  under your _____?
  NOUN

- Is your pet _____ afraid to come into your bedroom at
  ANIMAL

  _____ -time?
  NOUN

- Do you suspect something might be _____
  VERB ENDING IN "ING"

  all the _____ in your refrigerator while you
  TYPE OF FOOD (PLURAL)

  _____?
  VERB

- Do you find puddles of _____ _____
  ADJECTIVE   TYPE OF LIQUID

  around your bedroom?

If you answered "_____" to any of these questions, you
EXCLAMATION

have a/an _____ under your _____.
SOMETHING ALIVE   NOUN

MAD LIBS® is fun to play with friends, but you can also play it by yourself! To begin with, DO NOT look at the story on the page below. Fill in the blanks on this page with the words called for. Then, using the words you have selected, fill in the blank spaces in the story.

Now you've created your own hilarious MAD LIBS® game!

GET READY TO FLEA

SOMETHING ALIVE _____

PART OF THE BODY _____

ADJECTIVE _____

ADJECTIVE _____

VERB _____

SILLY WORD _____

ANIMAL _____

ADJECTIVE _____

ANIMAL (PLURAL) _____

TYPE OF LIQUID _____

ADJECTIVE _____

PLURAL NOUN _____

TYPE OF FOOD _____

PART OF THE BODY _____

NUMBER _____

VERB ENDING IN "ING" _____

PLURAL NOUN _____

A PLACE _____

MAD LIBS®

GET READY TO FLEA

Are you a were-_____ whose _____ gets
          SOMETHING ALIVE   PART OF THE BODY

itchy every time the moon is _____? You probably have
                              ADJECTIVE

a/an _____ case of werewolf fleas! But there's no need to
      ADJECTIVE

_____ in frustration—just go out and grab a bottle of
       VERB

Dr. _____'s werewolf _____ remover! Made with
     SILLY WORD   ANIMAL

the most _____ ingredients possible, our flea remover is
          ADJECTIVE

guaranteed to make all those itchy _____ disappear
                                      ANIMAL (PLURAL)

forever. Every bottle of flea remover contains a special blend of

_____ and _____-smelling _____ to
TYPE OF LIQUID   ADJECTIVE   PLURAL NOUN

make your fur as smooth as a/an _____ . Just pour some
                                 TYPE OF FOOD

of our flea remover on your _____ and wait _____
                            PART OF THE BODY   NUMBER

minutes. You'll be _____ with joy as you watch all
                   VERB ENDING IN "ING"

the _____ hop off your body so they never bother you
     PLURAL NOUN

again! Get howling and buy our werewolf flea remover at your local

_____ now!
  A PLACE

MAD LIBS® is fun to play with friends, but you can also play it by yourself! To begin with, DO NOT look at the story on the page below. Fill in the blanks on this page with the words called for. Then, using the words you have selected, fill in the blank spaces in the story.

Now you've created your own hilarious MAD LIBS® game!

MONSTER BASH

PLURAL NOUN _____

ANIMAL (PLURAL) _____

NOUN _____

OCCUPATION _____

PLURAL NOUN _____

VERB _____

ADJECTIVE _____

TYPE OF LIQUID _____

ADJECTIVE _____

TYPE OF FOOD (PLURAL) _____

OCCUPATION (PLURAL) _____

ADJECTIVE _____

PART OF THE BODY (PLURAL) _____

NOUN _____

ADJECTIVE _____

VERB _____

A PLACE _____

ARTICLE OF CLOTHING (PLURAL) _____

MAD LIBS®

MONSTER BASH

Listen up, all you creepy _____ and growling
PLURAL NOUN

_____! You're invited to Dr. _____'s Mad
ANIMAL (PLURAL) NOUN

_____ Monster Party! DJ Frankenmeyer will be in the
OCCUPATION

house spinning some awesome _____ , so be ready to
PLURAL NOUN

_____ all night long on the dance floor! All that fun is sure
VERB

to make you creatures of the night hungry for some _____
ADJECTIVE

snacks, so we'll be pouring _____ for all you wannabe
TYPE OF LIQUID

vampires and serving up platters of _____ deep-fried
ADJECTIVE

_____ for trolls and _____ alike! If you
TYPE OF FOOD (PLURAL) OCCUPATION (PLURAL)

want some _____ party games, we've got those, too. Get
ADJECTIVE

ready to bob for zombie _____ and pin the
PART OF THE BODY (PLURAL)

_____ on the werewolf! At the next _____ moon, fly,
NOUN ADJECTIVE

creep, or _____ to the castle on top of (the) _____
VERB A PLACE

and get ready to party until your _____ fall off!
ARTICLE OF CLOTHING (PLURAL)

MAD LIBS® is fun to play with friends, but you can also play it by yourself! To begin with, DO NOT look at the story on the page below. Fill in the blanks on this page with the words called for. Then, using the words you have selected, fill in the blank spaces in the story.

Now you've created your own hilarious MAD LIBS® game!

TOO CLOSE FOR COMFORT

ADJECTIVE _____

PART OF THE BODY (PLURAL) _____

VERB _____

SOMETHING ALIVE _____

PART OF THE BODY _____

ADJECTIVE _____

NOUN _____

PART OF THE BODY _____

NOUN _____

VERB _____

ADJECTIVE _____

VERB ENDING IN "ING" _____

NUMBER _____

ADJECTIVE _____

MAD LIBS

TOO CLOSE FOR COMFORT

Gilga the Hydra is interviewed for a web series on monsters:

Interviewer: It's _____ to meet you, Gilga. Tell me,
ADJECTIVE

what are some of the challenges of being a creature with seven

_____?
PART OF THE BODY (PLURAL)

Head #1: When we sleep, all the other heads _____ louder
VERB

than a/an _____ and keep me awake!
SOMETHING ALIVE

Head #2: Try being the _____ next to you! Your breath
PART OF THE BODY

smells like a/an _____ _____!
ADJECTIVE   NOUN

Head #7: Every time we eat, Head #3 chews with her _____
PART OF THE BODY

open!

Head #6: And Head #5 wants to be an internet _____, but
NOUN

she can't even _____!
VERB

Head #5: You're just _____ that I have a better
ADJECTIVE

_____ voice than you do!
VERB ENDING IN "ING"

Interviewer: Wow. I never knew having _____ heads could
NUMBER

be so _____!
ADJECTIVE

MAD LIBS® is fun to play with friends, but you can also play it by yourself! To begin with, DO NOT look at the story on the page below. Fill in the blanks on this page with the words called for. Then, using the words you have selected, fill in the blank spaces in the story.

Now you've created your own hilarious MAD LIBS® game!

SCARE STYLIST

ADJECTIVE _____

OCCUPATION _____

PART OF THE BODY _____

ADJECTIVE _____

ADJECTIVE _____

CELEBRITY _____

NOUN _____

ADVERB _____

NOUN _____

PLURAL NOUN _____

VERB (PAST TENSE) _____

NOUN _____

PART OF THE BODY _____

ANIMAL _____

PLURAL NOUN _____

ADJECTIVE _____

VERB _____

NOUN _____

MAD LIBS

SCARE STYLIST

Hello, my _____ monsters, and welcome to Medusa's
       ADJECTIVE

_____ video channel. If you have snakes growing out of
   OCCUPATION

your _____ like I do, then you'll learn all the most
    PART OF THE BODY

_____ ways to style them. If you want a/an _____
   ADJECTIVE   ADJECTIVE

look like _____ , just grab a/an _____ and use
         CELEBRITY   NOUN

it to _____ comb the snakes to the left before adding
      ADVERB

_____ gel to keep your snakes in place. If you want
   NOUN

something more old-fashioned, use _____ to curl your
                                   PLURAL NOUN

snakes, and you'll look like you just _____ out of a
                                      VERB (PAST TENSE)

fashion _____! And if you're looking for something more
        NOUN

daring, use _____ spray to hold your snakes straight up
            PART OF THE BODY

in a mo-_____ style. Of course, the key to any good style
        ANIMAL

is to feed your snakes _____ to keep them looking
                        PLURAL NOUN

_____ and happy. And whatever you do, don't _____
   ADJECTIVE   VERB

at yourself in a mirror, because if you do, your snakes will turn you

into a granite _____!
               NOUN

MAD LIBS® is fun to play with friends, but you can also play it by yourself! To begin with, DO NOT look at the story on the page below. Fill in the blanks on this page with the words called for. Then, using the words you have selected, fill in the blank spaces in the story.

Now you've created your own hilarious MAD LIBS® game!

HOW TO KNOW IF YOU'VE BEEN BITTEN BY A VAMPIRE

PART OF THE BODY _____

PLURAL NOUN _____

ADJECTIVE _____

LAST NAME _____

SOMETHING ALIVE (PLURAL) _____

TYPE OF LIQUID _____

VERB _____

NOUN _____

NOUN _____

ADVERB _____

PART OF THE BODY (PLURAL) _____

PLURAL NOUN _____

OCCUPATION (PLURAL) _____

NOUN _____

PART OF THE BODY _____

NUMBER _____

NOUN _____

Have you recently been bitten on the _____ by a bat?
PART OF THE BODY

Answer these _____ to find out if the _____ bat
PLURAL NOUN   ADJECTIVE

that bit you is really a vampire!

- Have you started to introduce yourself as Count _____?
  LAST NAME

  If so, do you have the sudden urge to bite _____
  SOMETHING ALIVE (PLURAL)

  and suck their _____?
  TYPE OF LIQUID

- Do you _____ during the day in a wooden
  VERB

  _____ or do you transform into a/an _____
  NOUN   NOUN

  when you _____ flap your _____?
  ADVERB   PART OF THE BODY (PLURAL)

- Do you only want to wear black _____?
  PLURAL NOUN

- Do _____ keep trying to drive a wooden
  OCCUPATION (PLURAL)

  _____ into your _____?
  NOUN   PART OF THE BODY

If you answered "yes" to more than _____ of these questions,
NUMBER

better get out of the sun—you just might be a/an _____!
NOUN

MAD LIBS® is fun to play with friends, but you can also play it by yourself! To begin with, DO NOT look at the story on the page below. Fill in the blanks on this page with the words called for. Then, using the words you have selected, fill in the blank spaces in the story.

Now you've created your own hilarious MAD LIBS® game!

YETI OR NOT

SILLY WORD _____

ADJECTIVE _____

NOUN _____

A PLACE _____

OCCUPATION (PLURAL) _____

NUMBER _____

NOUN _____

PART OF THE BODY _____

ADVERB _____

VERB _____

SOMETHING ALIVE _____

NOUN _____

ANIMAL _____

ADJECTIVE _____

NOUN _____

PLURAL NOUN _____

ARTICLE OF CLOTHING _____

NOUN _____

MAD LIBS

YETI OR NOT

Welcome to Mount _____ , home to a/an _____
                    SILLY WORD   ADJECTIVE

creature known as the abominable _____ -man. It is also
                                        NOUN

known as the yeti, which translates to "_____ bear." Many
                                            A PLACE

_____ who have climbed the snow-covered mountain
OCCUPATION (PLURAL)

claim to have seen the yeti. They say the yeti stands _____
                                                            NUMBER

feet tall, is covered in white _____ , and leaves huge
                                      NOUN

_____ -prints in the snow. Yetis are _____ shy
PART OF THE BODY   ADVERB

creatures, so they'll always run and _____ when someone sees
                                          VERB

them. A yeti's favorite place to hide is behind a/an _____ .
                                                    SOMETHING ALIVE

A yeti's favorite activities are _____ -ball fights with its
                                        NOUN

_____ friends and sledding down the mountain on a/an
    ANIMAL

_____ _____ . Since the mountain is always covered
ADJECTIVE   NOUN

in _____ , even in the summer, make sure to wear a warm
    PLURAL NOUN

_____ if you go searching for the yeti. And bring a/an
ARTICLE OF CLOTHING

_____ to take plenty of photos!
    NOUN

MAD LIBS® is fun to play with friends, but you can also play it by yourself! To begin with, DO NOT look at the story on the page below. Fill in the blanks on this page with the words called for. Then, using the words you have selected, fill in the blank spaces in the story.

Now you've created your own hilarious MAD LIBS® game!

AN EYE FOR TROUBLE

ADJECTIVE _____

PART OF THE BODY _____

NOUN _____

SAME PART OF THE BODY _____

ADJECTIVE _____

SOMETHING ALIVE (PLURAL) _____

ADJECTIVE _____

A PLACE _____

PLURAL NOUN _____

ADJECTIVE _____

VERB _____

A PLACE _____

VERB _____

OCCUPATION (PLURAL) _____

PLURAL NOUN _____

PLURAL NOUN _____

NUMBER _____

VERB ENDING IN "ING" _____

AN EYE FOR TROUBLE

Being a cyclops isn't always as _____ as it seems. The first

ADJECTIVE

problem is that I only have one _____ . It gets really

PART OF THE BODY

difficult to see when my _____ grows too long and hangs

NOUN

down over my _____ . But the most _____

SAME PART OF THE BODY   ADJECTIVE

problem I have is all the _____ living at the

SOMETHING ALIVE (PLURAL)

bottom of my mountain. Every month or so, they get all _____

ADJECTIVE

and come marching up to my _____ waving torches and

A PLACE

_____ . They shout _____ things like

PLURAL NOUN   ADJECTIVE

" _____ the cyclops!" Usually when they storm up, I just

VERB

stomp out of my _____ and _____ loudly a few

A PLACE   VERB

times. This scares most of the _____ away, but some of

OCCUPATION (PLURAL)

them always try to stab me with their _____ . I usually

PLURAL NOUN

throw a few _____ at them to make the rest of the people

PLURAL NOUN

run away, too. Maybe if I had _____ eyes instead of just

NUMBER

one, the villagers would leave me alone, but until that day, I'll just keep

_____ them when they bother me.

VERB ENDING IN "ING"

MAD LIBS® is fun to play with friends, but you can also play it by yourself! To begin with, DO NOT look at the story on the page below. Fill in the blanks on this page with the words called for. Then, using the words you have selected, fill in the blank spaces in the story.

Now you've created your own hilarious MAD LIBS® game!

DON'T LOSE YOUR HEAD

NOUN _____

ADJECTIVE _____

OCCUPATION _____

NOUN _____

ADJECTIVE _____

ADJECTIVE _____

PLURAL NOUN _____

NOUN _____

PART OF THE BODY _____

ADVERB _____

SOMETHING ALIVE _____

NOUN _____

SOMETHING ALIVE (PLURAL) _____

ADJECTIVE _____

ADJECTIVE _____

NOUN _____

VERB ENDING IN "ING" _____

MAD LIBS

DON'T LOSE YOUR HEAD

An interview with the Headless Horseman:

Interviewer: Welcome to "Interview with a/an _____."
NOUN

Today we'll be interviewing a/an _____ creature, the
ADJECTIVE

Headless _____ ! Your fans are wondering, what's it like
OCCUPATION

having a/an _____ for a head?
NOUN

Headless Horseman: It's absolutely _____ . First I had to dig
ADJECTIVE

out all the _____ _____ that were inside it. Then
ADJECTIVE PLURAL NOUN

I used a/an _____ to carve a new _____ . On dark
NOUN PART OF THE BODY

nights, I'll _____ ride around on my _____ ,
ADVERB SOMETHING ALIVE

take off my _____ , and throw it at _____
NOUN SOMETHING ALIVE (PLURAL)

to scare them!

Interviewer: Sounds _____ !
ADJECTIVE

Headless Horseman: But the most _____ part of being the
ADJECTIVE

Headless Horseman is that I never have to buy a/an _____ to
NOUN

wear when I go trick-or-_____ on Halloween!
VERB ENDING IN "ING"

From MONSTER MASH MAD LIBS® • Copyright © 2021 by Penguin Random House LLC.